QUALITY INTERVIEWING:
THIRD EDITION

Robert B. Maddux

CRISP PUBLICATIONS, INC.
Menlo Park, California

QUALITY INTERVIEWING:

THIRD EDITION

CREDITS
Editor: **Michael G. Crisp**
Layout & Composition: **Interface Studio**
Cover Design: **Carol Harris**
Artwork: **Ralph Mapson**

Copyright © 1986, 1988, 1994 by Crisp Publications, Inc.
Printed in the United States of America

Distribution to the U.S. Trade:

National Book Network, Inc.
4720 Boston Way
Lanham, MD 20706
1-800-462-6420

Distribution to the Canadian Trade:

Raincoast Books
8680 Cambie Street
Vancouver, B.C.
V6P 6M9
604-323-7100
800-663-5714

Library of Congress Catalog Card Number 93-07049
Maddux, Robert B.
Quality Interviewing: Third Edition
ISBN 1-56052-262-3

This book is printed on recyclable paper with soy ink.

PREFACE

This book is for anyone interested in learning job interview techniques, especially those who select others to work with them. Whether an employment interviewer, first line supervisor, chairperson of a committee, project leader, school administrator, restaurant manager, government official, owner of a small business, or senior executive, you must be able to assess candidates and arrive at the best choice.

Although resumes, recommendations and applications are important, the interview is the most critical element in the selection process. It may last no longer than twenty or thirty minutes, yet it is the best means available to obtain the information you need from an applicant. As interviewer, your job is to gather facts, solicit opinions and form impressions in order to predict the performance of the individual you select for the position you are seeking to fill. It is not an overstatement to say that interviewing controls the ultimate success of an organization because it determines the level of talent within it.

This book is designed to help you think through the selection process, and learn to conduct interviews that will lead to sound decisions based on your pre-determined specifications. Those who master good interviewing skills will greatly improve the quality of their organizations.

This book should be read with a pencil since you will be encouraged to complete a number of exercises which apply the concepts presented. You will also have a chance to do some self-analysis which will help you identify personal strengths and weaknesses. Once learned, the application of the skills is up to you.

GOOD LUCK!

Robert B. Maddux

ABOUT THIS BOOK

QUALITY INTERVIEWING is not like most books. It stands out from other self-help books in an important way. It's not a book to read—it's a book to *use*. The unique "self-paced" format of this book and the many worksheets, encourage a reader to get involved and, try some new ideas immediately.

This book will introduce the basic concepts of conducting a professional job interview. Using the simple yet sound techniques presented can make a dramatic change in the overall success of any organization.

QUALITY INTERVIEWING can be used effectively in a number of ways. Here are some posibilities:

—Individual Study. Because the book is self-instructional, all that is needed is a quiet place, some time and a pencil. By completing the activities and exercises, a reader should receive practical ideas on how to conduct a quality job interview.

—Workshops and Seminars. The book is ideal for assigned reading *prior to* a workshop or seminar. With the basics in hand, the quality of the participation will improve, and more time can be spent on concept extensions and applications during the program. The book is also effective when it is distributed at the beginning of a session, and participants "work through" the contents.

—Remote Location Training. Books can be sent to those not able to attend "home office" training sessions.

There are several other possibilities that depend on the objectives, program or ideas of the user.

One thing for sure, even after it has been read, this book will be looked at—and thought about—again and again.

CONTENTS

PART I

PLANNING FOR THE INTERVIEW

SOME IMPORTANT OBJECTIVES FOR THE READER

Before you begin this book, give some thought to your objectives.

Objectives give us a sense of direction; a definition of what we plan to accomplish; and a feeling of fulfillment when they are achieved.

Check the objectives below that are important to you. Then, when you have completed the book, review your objectives and enjoy the sense of achievement you will feel.

AFTER LEARNING AND PRACTICING CONCEPTS PRESENTED IN THIS BOOK, YOU WILL BE ABLE TO:

☐ properly plan and prepare for an employment interview.

☐ create a climate for communication.

☐ direct the interview so maximum pertinent information is obtained from the applicant.

☐ provide appropriate information for the applicant.

☐ evaluate the candidate's qualifications against bonafide job requirements.

☐ promote good will whether or not the applicant is hired.

4

EQUAL EMPLOYMENT OPPORTUNITY CONSIDERATIONS

Legislation during the past few years has had a dramatic impact on the selection process. Anyone interviewing job candidates must be conscious of areas in which seemingly innocent actions or questions can subject the organization to charges of discrimination. The next page provides some examples of unlawful practices.

The purpose of equal opportunity legislation is to focus placement decisions on the applicant's ability to do a given job based on knowledge, experience, and skill rather than some arbitrary criteria unrelated to work requirements.

This book was written with these considerations in mind. Readers are cautioned, however, to seek counsel regarding selection practices in their organizations. This is important because both State and Federal laws are subject to frequent revisions, interpretations, and judicial decisions.

SOME UNLAWFUL PRACTICES

ILLEGAL EMPLOYMENT PRACTICES

Legislation covering equal employment opportunity is extensive and complex. Therefore, only the rudiments of unlawful selection practices can be highlighted here.

Copies of Local, State, and Federal laws can be obtained from the appropriate governmental agency. Also, most organizations have individuals who specialize in the interpretation and application of these laws. They are anxious to help when you have questions or problems.

The following practices reflect the thrust of current legislation and the dangers inherent in careless interview and selection techniques. Check ☑ those you need to learn more about, then make sure you get the help you need.

UNDER CURRENT LEGISLATION IT IS UNLAWFUL TO:

☐ 1. Refuse to consider for employment, or otherwise discriminate against any person because of race, color, national origin, sex, religion, physical disability or age.

☐ 2. Show a bias in help-wanted advertising for or against applicants based on race, color, national origin, sex, religion or age unless you can prove your requirements are bonafide occupational qualifications.

☐ 3. Use any screening techniques for employment or promotion, i.e., paper and pencil tests, questionnaires, etc., that cannot be proved to be directly job related.

☐ 4. Categorize job candidates on the basis of race, color, national origin, sex, religion or age.

☐ 5. Ask about previous mental and physical disabilities during an interview.

☐ 6. Refuse to hire a woman because separate facilities would have to be provided. Nor can an employer refuse to hire a woman because he would have to pay her special benefits, i.e., premium overtime, rest periods, etc., required by State law. (Note: An employer would have to give men the same benefits as women. Discrimination is a two-way street).

☐ 7. Perpetuate past discriminatory practices that have led to statistical imbalances in the workforce.

☐ 8. Use polygraphs, voice print devices and other related technology in the selection of employees.

ILLEGAL EMPLOYMENT PRACTICES
(Continued)

☐ 9. Seek facts which may indirectly reveal the applicant's race, color, religion or national origin. Such facts include, but are not limited to, the following:

- The applicants original name when the name has been legally changed.

- The applicant's birthplace (i.e., country, city, part of town, etc.) or the birthplace of the applicants relatives. You can ask if the applicant is a US Citizen. If he/she isn't a citizen you'll need to determine if the applicant has a work visa.

- Citizenship of the applicants parents.

- The nature of the applicant's "first" language, if English is a "second" language, or the means by which the applicant acquired a foreign language as a "second" language. If you are concerned about a language problem, you can ask about the applicant's proficiency in reading English, provided such a proficiency is related to job performance.

- The applicants religious background, religious affiliations or religious activities.

- The applicant's membership in organizations, clubs, societies, etc.

☐ 10. Request information about police records or arrest records that the applicant may have which have not resulted in convictions. Even if the applicant has been convicted, unless the crime raises questions about the applicant's potential job performance (i.e., applicant was convicted of embezzlement and is applying for a job as a treasurer,) this information cannot be used to reject the applicant.

SEE APPENDIX A FOR SPECIFIC EXAMPLES OF QUESTIONS THAT ARE EITHER CONSIDERED ILLEGAL OR COULD BE CONSTRUED TO REFLECT A PATTERN OF DISCRIMINATION.

TESTING CONSIDERATIONS

If testing is used as part of the screening process, it should serve a well defined purpose. Testing for the sake of testing is expensive and legally dangerous. There must be a clear understanding of desired outcomes and the role they will play in the selection decision.

Three major considerations in the use of testing are legality, cost and organizational commitment to intelligent usage and interpretation.

LEGALITY

All paper and pencil testing must pass scrutiny in terms of validity, business necessity and adverse impact. Validity means that the test measures what it purports to measure. Packaged tests for personality, skills and honesty have been validated by the developer. The user, however, must be very sure they are testing a comparable population under comparable conditions.

The employer must also be able to demonstrate that the skills or characteristics measured are a business necessity. For instance, you may not require a laborer to pass a mathematics test unless you can show solving mathematical problems is a requirement of the job.

The following are important considerations in drug testing:

- There are no federal laws regulating drug screening.
- Currently, California, Connecticut, Iowa, Minnesota and Vermont are the only states with laws regulating drug screening although several are debating it. Review your plans with a legal expert in this area before implementing a drug screening program.
- Employers within the jurisdiction of federal, state or local antidiscrimination regulations may risk disparate impact. (The screening has an unfair impact on one or more protected classes of applicants.)
- The initiation of a drug screening program must be included in collective bargaining.

Physical screening must also measure what it purports to measure. The test must be shown to be a business necessity and must not have a disparate impact on protected groups.

COSTS

Costs vary greatly depending upon the types of screening activities undertaken and the size of the potential applicant base to which they will be applied. Appropriate research should be undertaken to project costs prior to making an organizational commitment to a testing program.

ORGANIZATIONAL COMMITMENT

The organization must closely examine its motive for testing. What is its purpose? What precipitated it? What are the expected results? Is there a commitment to close monitoring and confidentiality? Is there an equally effective alternative?

Interviewing is an important task and must be done well.

It is also expensive. It is estimated, on the average, that it costs about $5,000 to replace a clerical person and approximately $20,000 to replace a professional or manager. These costs include recruitment expense, plus the loss of productivity while a job is vacant and/or a replacement is being trained.

Some people are very successful interviewers, others are failures. See the next page for a contrast of the two.

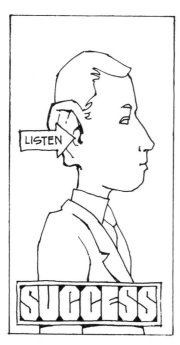

MEET SOME SUCCESSES AND FAILURES

SUCCESSES	FAILURES
Those who do a thorough analysis of job requirements in advance.	Those who rely on memory for job requirements.
Interviewers who compare qualifications on the application with the job requirements, prior to the interview.	People who examine applications only superficially before the interview.
Interviewers who develop a logical plan in advance based on information required to make a selection decision.	Interviewers who interview without a plan.
Those who get applicants to talk freely, and listen while they do so.	Those who do most of the talking and very little listening.
Interviewers who adhere to equal employment opportunity guidelines.	Interviewers who disregard the legal implications of their actions.
Those who evaluate the facts, and avoid premature conclusions and stereotyping.	Those heavily influenced by characteristics that are not job related.
Those who make selection decisions based on the applicant's qualifications and ability to handle the job requirements.	People who make job selections casually with limited consideration of qualifications versus job requirements.
Add From Your Own Experience:	Add From Your Own Experience:

NEVER UNDERESTIMATE THE IMPORTANCE OF THE SELECTION INTERVIEW.

The interview is <u>the</u> critical communications link in the selection process. It should meet the needs of the applicant as well as those of the hiring organization. The interviewer and the applicant will form important and lasting impressions of each other from the interview. Applicants who appear reluctant to provide pertinent information about experience and skills will be dismissed as serious candidates. The applicants interest will be diminished by employers who seem unenthusiastic about the position and reluctant to talk about it and the organization.

See the next page for specifics.

THE SELECTION INTERVIEW

THE IMPORTANCE OF THE SELECTION INTERVIEW

Several aspects of the selection interview are listed below. Check ☑ those you agree are vital.

☐ 1. The interview must provide adequate information about the applicant's education, formal training, skills, work experience, performance in previous positions, plus personal characteristics (such as attitude, ability to communicate, etc.). This information will help you determine the interviewee's ability to do the job.

☐ 2. Good performance in one organization does not automatically assure the same performance in another. The interview, therefore, must determine not only if the candidate can do the job, but also whether that person is anxious to perform it well in your organization.

☐ 3. An applicant needs to learn basic job requirements plus other facts about your organization in order to make an intelligent decision. This information includes items such as: job description; hours of work; compensation; benefits coverage; and opportunities for personal growth.

☐ 4. The interview should promote good-will between the candidate and your organization regardless of whether it ends with employment or not.

EVERY PERSON WHO INTERVIEWS AN APPLICANT SHOULD REALIZE HIS/HER APPROACH WILL HEAVILY INFLUENCE THE OUTCOME.

INTERVIEW STYLES

Every interviewer brings a different personality to the interview depending on background and experience. This individual style, however, must be blended into an effective interviewing format if the outcome is to be successful. Several styles are described on the next page. Check ✔ the one which best fits you.

INTERVIEW STYLES

Five interview styles are listed below. Four generally produce poor results and should be avoided. Which one most closely resembles your current style?

☐ 1. **THE "EYEBALL" INTERVIEW**—"I knew the minute I saw her she couldn't handle the job." In this style, interviewers assume they can predict job performance on the basis of appearance, handshake and other cursory observations. It is very superficial and totally unreliable.

☐ 2. **THE FRIENDLY CHAT**—It can be a pleasant experience talking about sports, the weather, mutual experiences, etc. Unless controlled, however, the business purpose of the interview will never be achieved.

☐ 3. **THE INQUISITION**—Some interviewers enjoy placing an applicant under stress to see how they react. The usual result is withdrawal by the candidate. Accordingly, little is learned about ability or performance.

☐ 4. **THE STRAIGHT DOWN THE MIDDLE INTERVIEW**—The interviewer will ask a predetermined series of questions in a standard order. This interview is so stiff and inflexible that it does not permit the interviewer to explore areas of potential mutual interest. It also limits the candidate's expression of qualifications and personality.

☐ 5. **THE BUSINESSLIKE INTERVIEW**—This interview is a social situation with a business purpose in which worthwhile information is exchanged between the parties. It does not begin until the interviewer has clear understanding of the responsibilities of the job to be filled and an idea of the kind of person required to fulfill them.

This style is endorsed in this book.

DID YOU CHECK ✔ THE STYLE YOU USE MOST OFTEN?

PERSONAL SKILLS REVIEW

Selection interviewing is not a daily task for most people. Consequently they get very little practice. If they have not had special training, or made an effort to learn on their own, the results will be poor.

Therefore, before we look at the selection interview process in detail, you might find it worthwhile to assess your interviewing skills. Do this on the next page.

ASSESS YOURSELF

INTERVIEWER'S SELF-ASSESSMENT

The following personal characteristics are important for professional interviewers. The scale will help identify your strengths, and determine areas where improvements may be necessary. Circle the number that best reflects where you fall on the scale. The higher the number, the more like the characteristic you feel you are. When you have finished, total the numbers circled in the space provided.

1.	I analyze job requirements thoroughly before beginning the selection process.	5	4	3	2	1
2.	I study qualifications of applicants in light of the job requirements before each interview.	5	4	3	2	1
3.	I develop a unique interview plan based on the activity in item 2.	5	4	3	2	1
4.	I begin each interview by establishing a relaxed climate conducive to good communication.	5	4	3	2	1
5.	I make an effort to get the applicant to talk freely.	5	4	3	2	1
6.	I use questions to draw out essential information.	5	4	3	2	1
7.	I listen more than I talk.	5	4	3	2	1
8.	I avoid preconception and personal bias.	5	4	3	2	1
9.	I adhere to equal employment opportunity guidelines.	5	4	3	2	1
10.	I record key points.	5	4	3	2	1
11.	I provide information about the job, and the organization, and answer the applicant's questions.	5	4	3	2	1
12.	I make selection decisions on the basis of job requirements.	5	4	3	2	1
13.	I document my selection decisions.	5	4	3	2	1
14.	I let all candidates know the outcome of their interview at the appropriate time.	5	4	3	2	1

TOTAL _____

A score between 56 and 70 suggests you probably conduct successful interviews. Scores between 42 and 55 indicate some significant strengths as well as some improvement needs. A score below 42 calls for a serious effort to improve in a number of areas. Make a special effort to improve in any area where you scored 3 or less regardless of your total score.

**SELECTION INTERVIEWS CAN
BE COMPARED TO BASEBALL**

- Every interview requires a game plan.
- Winning depends on advance preparation and the application of acquired skills.
- Each player needs a turn at bat.
- Four basic essentials (bases) need to be covered to achieve the best results.
- There may be several outs before a run is scored.
- The rules are enforced by an umpire.

REMEMBER TO TOUCH THE BASES

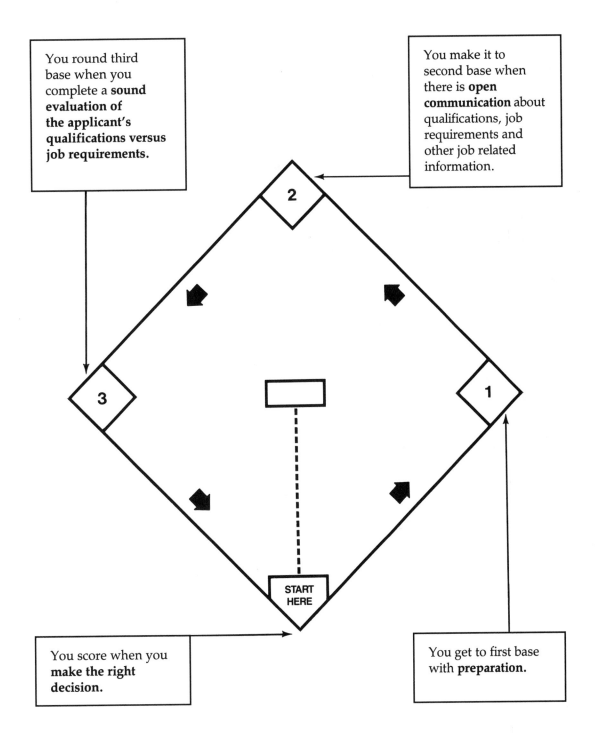

You round third base when you complete a **sound evaluation of the applicant's qualifications versus job requirements.**

You make it to second base when there is **open communication** about qualifications, job requirements and other job related information.

2

3

1

START HERE

You score when you **make the right decision.**

You get to first base with **preparation.**

WHAT IS THE FIRST THING
YOU SHOULD DO WHEN
YOU HAVE A VACANT POSITION?

The best first step is to determine whether the vacancy needs to be filled. If the answer is ''yes'', the next question should be, ''what qualifications are required for a replacement?'' The answer requires a review of the job itself. The next three pages tell you how to approach this task systematically.

HOW TO DETERMINE JOB REQUIREMENTS

A fundamental step in finding the best candidate is to determine the job requirements of the position to be filled. Unfortunately, this is frequently overlooked. Supervisors often believe they know all aspects of each position and evaluate applicants accordingly. Often they simply look for someone *like* the person being replaced. They do not consider what might be achieved by a person with different qualifications who might better fit the actual job requirements. A thorough review of job requirements helps refresh and remind a supervisor of ways in which the job may have changed. If it has changed enough, it may be better performed by a person with different qualifications.

HIRING DECISIONS BASED ON UNFOUNDED ASSUMPTIONS ARE A LEADING CAUSE OF POOR SELECTION.

If a formal position description is not available; one should be prepared.

Information about the job will fall into the following five categories:

☐ 1. **THE PURPOSE OF THE JOB:**
- What is the ultimate product or service desired?
- What is the relationship of this job to others in the organization?
- What are the consequences of poor, or non-performance?

☐ 2. **WHAT THE JOB HOLDER ACTUALLY DOES:**

- What are the most important duties performed?

- What are the secondary duties?

- How often are the duties performed?

- What is the nature and scope of decision making?

☐ 3. **HOW THE PERSON PERFORMS THE JOB:**

- What are the reporting relationships?

- What internal and external contacts are involved?

- What are the general working conditions (i.e. place, hours, hazards, advantages, co-workers)?

☐ 4. **WHAT HUMAN RELATIONS AND PERSONAL SKILLS ARE REQUIRED:**

- What interpersonal skills are required to support relationships with others?

- Is the position detail oriented?

- Is logic or reasoning required?

- What specific skills are absolutely essential?

- Is good grooming required?

- How important is attitude?

☐ 5. **WHAT PHYSICAL ATTRIBUTES ARE NECESSARY:**

- Is physical strength required?

- Is size a factor?

> Note: Physical characteristics must be bonafide. If you elect not to hire a handicapped person, you may be required to show:
> - specifically how the handicap prevents the person from doing the work.
> - how the person would create a health or safety hazard for others.

CRITICAL PERFORMANCE FACTORS

Once key elements of the position have been established, critical performance factors should be identified.

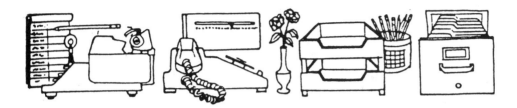

A position classified "material coordinator" might be approached in the following way.

Knowledge requirements can be determined by examining the job structure, the type of materials coordinated, and the personal interfaces involved.

If records must be maintained on incoming and outgoing materials, they can be reviewed to determine the clerical skills required and the amount of detail involved.

An examination of the type and scope of person to person transactions (and the conditions under which they occur), will determine the interpersonal skills requirements of the position.

Observing the actual worksite and performance of the work being done will determine the physical attributes the work demands.

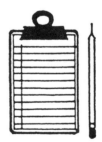

ESTABLISHING QUALIFICATIONS

Minimum hiring qualifications for a position should be drawn directly from the job requirements. If it is an entry position, the potential of an individual to progress should be considered, but unreasonable qualifications should not be demanded for a new hire. For example, a college degree for an entry level secretarial position is unrealistic. The possibility of an individual progressing to an assignment where a degree would be helpful does not justify this requirement at entry level.

A job specification worksheet like the one on the next page is one way to establish the required qualifications.

JOB SPECIFICATION WORKSHEET

JOB SPECIFICATION WORKSHEET

Prepare a job specification worksheet similar to this prior to the actual interview.

1. List the most critical responsibilities of the job (make or break factors).

    EXAMPLE: | Typist/Community Health Education |

    > Typing
    > Filing
    > Mail processing and distribution
    > Completing administrative reports
    > Answering telephones and receiving visitors

2. List the duties critical to the performance of each major responsibility.

    EXAMPLE: | Typing |

    > Type general correspondence
    > Type monthly activity reports
    > Type copy for brochures
    > Type statistical tables

3. List the critical skills and knowledge necessary to perform each duty.

    EXAMPLE: **Type correspondence—55 wpm error free**

    Type copy for brochures—do page layout
    Type statistical summaries—understand basic math
    Draft general correspondence—be able to write clearly

4. List degree of skill required and whether it is mandatory, desired or will be taught.

    EXAMPLE: **Typing—55 wpm straight copy—mandatory**

    Typing—30 wpm unarranged rough draft—desirable
    Spelling and grammar—error free—mandatory
    Basic math skills—mandatory
    Page layout—will train

5. List expected results.

    EXAMPLE: **Type attractive error free documents that communicate clearly and concisely.**

6. List the physical attributes necessary to perform the job.

    EXAMPLE: **Normal stooping and bending.**
    Read fine print.
    Hear well enough to handle telephones.

7. List the behavioral attributes necessary to perform the job.

    EXAMPLE: **Daily communication with large numbers of diverse personalities. Must be cheerful and communicative.**

CASE STUDIES

Case studies help provide insights. Four case problems are included in this book. Please give each your careful attention.

The first case (on the facing page) can help you understand the importance of reviewing job specifications before beginning the selection process.

CASE 1

MARY ANN'S
REPLACEMENT PROBLEM

Mary Ann was promoted to supervisor of the computer services unit two weeks ago. She worked in this unit when it was first formed (five years ago) but for the past three years she has been working with another group. The functions of the computer service unit have changed greatly during the past five years.

Yesterday, one of Mary Ann's senior service representatives announced his decision to retire at the end of the month. Mary Ann is anxious to begin the search for a replacement but is not sure where to start. Which of the following initial actions would you recommend she take. Check ☑ any or all you feel would apply.

☐ Begin an immediate search for candidates.

☐ Review (and update if necessary) the job description for the position in question.

☐ Review staffing versus workload for the entire unit to determine if the position is still needed.

☐ Review the knowledge and skills currently required in the position and weigh them against any changes in function that are planned for the future.

☐ Discuss job knowledge and skill requirements with the incumbent. What are considered to be the most critical?

☐ Ask other departments serviced if their needs are being fully met by the skills and knowledge of the existing staff?

☐ Examine the possibility of reassigning existing staff members for either cross training or promotion.

Compare your answers with those of the author on page 66.

Placement decisions should be based on an applicant's ability to do a given job as demonstrated by knowledge, skills, desire, experience and attitude.

Just as a baseball player coming to bat takes a few practice swings, the interviewer must prepare a general plan prior to beginning the interview in order to elicit the information needed to make an appropriate comparison of job specifications and applicant qualifications.

You will be at first base once you complete the exercise on the facing page. You will make it to second when both parties communicate freely about job requirements, job qualifications, and other related information. It takes some skill!

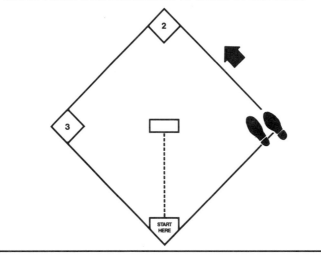

HOW TO PREPARE AN INTERVIEW ACTION PLAN FOR EACH APPLICANT

After the job specification worksheet has been completed and updated, the interviewer should prepare an action plan for each interview. The following steps will help accomplish this:

☐ 1. Study the applicant's general qualifications and work history from the employment application and/or resume. (The job specification work sheet will probably be helpful as a guide). Determine what additional information, or clarification is required. Decide what questions will fill any information gaps. Be sure to include the ''make'' or ''break'' questions you plan to ask every candidate to assure consistency in evaluating qualifications against job requirements.

> **Know what you want before you begin the interview.**

☐ 2. Make a list of other questions you want the applicant to answer. Keep these handy to insure they will not be overlooked during the interview.

☐ 3. Review what information about the job and organization you will need to provide to the candidate. (See Appendix B for tips.)

☐ 4. Arrange for a private place, away from noise and other distractions, to conduct the interview.

☐ 5. Take steps to avoid interruptions during the interview.

> Check ✔ those items you do well.

28

PART II

CONDUCTING A QUALITY INTERVIEW

GAINING THE APPLICANT'S COOPERATION AND CONFIDENCE

An interview is essentially a social process and should be conducted accordingly. The tone should be pleasant, but business-like. A good interview is designed to gain the cooperation and confidence of the interviewee. Professional interviewers do the following. Check ☑ those items you agree are important.

☐ 1. **Be on time.** This is just like any other business appointment.

☐ 2. **Treat applicants the same.** The way you greet and talk with applicants may be interpreted as a signal of good or ill will, and could invite charges of discrimination if your manner was inconsistent.

☐ 3. **Establish rapport.** Strive for a relaxed yet business-like atmosphere conducive to open communication.

☐ 4. **Be sincere.** Show a genuine interest in the applicant.

☐ 5. **Show respect for the individual.** Give each person your attention and listen to his or her views even though their value system may be different from your own.

☐ 6. **Provide information.** The candidate needs information on which to determine his or her interest in the job. Answer questions, and when appropriate provide specific information about the job, working conditions, compensation, benefits as well as the expectations and goals of your organization.

☐ 7. **Explain the placement process.** Don't leave people guessing. Tell them the purpose of the interview and what the next steps will be. Let them know when you expect to make a final decision.

The goal of each interview is to gather pertinent information in order to make the best possible decision about an applicant's ability to do a specific job. This information may include:

- Work Experience.

- Personal Goals.

- Education.

- Evidence of Dependability.

- Technical, Analytical, Clerical, or Manual Skills and Knowledge.

- Attitude.

- Hobbies and Other Interests.

- Past Achievements.

The following pages suggest ways to obtain this information.

HOW TO GATHER JOB RELATED DATA FROM APPLICANT'S

An interviewer needs to determine how a candidate will function in everyday job activities. Methods to gather this information must be job-centered and pursued without discrimination. Questions should stimulate the applicant to respond naturally. Ways in which this can be done include the following. Check ☑ those you feel you are using, or will learn to use effectively.

☐ 1. **Ask general, open-ended questions that do not suggest a particular answer.**
   "Could you tell me a little about how you got that promotion?" will tell you more about what the person considers important than "Do you like your job?" Another useful open-ended technique is to follow an answer with "What happened then?" or "What did you do next?"

☐ 2. **Use short questions.**
   The more words you use in a question, the more likely you are to influence the answer. If the applicant says, "I thought the group I worked with was excellent." you might say, "What made the group in which you worked excellent?" A better response would be "In what sense?", or "How so?" The applicant is more apt to react in a normal way since there is nothing in the question that requires evaluation or suggests a particular response.

   Spontaneity often yields what an applicant *really* feels.

HOW TO GATHER JOB RELATED DATA
(Continued)

☐ 3. **Listen carefully to each response; then decide on your next question.**
A good interviewer spends nearly 80 percent of the time listening.
Many inexperienced interviewers are in such a hurry to get to the next
question, they fail to hear the applicant's response. Listen attentively
to each answer. Often an answer will determine the next question.
If the response does not provide enough information, say, ''tell me
more''; or ''can you be more specific?''. If the information is adequate
for the question being asked; go on with the interview plan.

> AN INTERVIEWER LEARNS MORE FROM LISTENING
> THAN TALKING!

☐ 4. **Probe the candidate's range of expertise.**
Ask applicants basic, fundamental questions about their field of
expertise. Interviewers should not try to demonstrate equal or superior
knowledge to a candidate (even if they possess it). The best responses
are given freely and normally. Those which are guarded or tentative
because an applicant fears the level of the interviewer's expertise will
be difficult to evaluate.

☐ 5. **Stimulate value judgments.**
Asking a candidate how he or she feels about punctuality; conduct
on the job; personal commitment to a task or relationships with
previous co-workers will help provide insights in that person's value
system. This information is more valuable when evaluating a candidate
than an interviewer's ''assumptions''.

HOW TO GATHER JOB RELATED DATA
(Continued)

☐ 6. **Probe "choice points".**
"Choice points" are situations which require the applicant to explain why they selected one course of action over another. For example, why they majored in business instead of engineering. Listening to reasons why a choice was made, can help provide insights to the individual's reasoning and value system.

☐ 7. **Use silence effectively.**
Some interviewers become uncomfortable when silence occurs during an interview and feel compelled to talk. Silence provides time to think (which is often what the applicant is doing). Interviewers who wait out the silence while looking expectantly at the interviewee will learn more than those who don't. An applicant, sensing more information is desired, will often provide more pertinent information than anticipated.

☐ 8. **Use reflective statements.**
Reflecting comments back to a candidate is a good technique. It shows you were listening, and wish to stimulate elaboration of an answer. This must be done in a natural way which shows interest or concern. Here is an example:

APPLICANT: I was pretty excited over the special assignment!

INTERVIEWER: You were pretty excited about the project?

APPLICANT: Sure, it was the one I had worked to achieve and one I felt I had earned.

INTERVIEWER: You felt you had earned it?

APPLICANT: I went to school for six months at night to qualify.

INTERVIEWER: Six months?

APPLICANT: That's right. Three nights a week and three hours a night.

You're making good progress toward second base. Now is a good time to apply what you have read. Analyze the case study on the next page using some of what you have learned.

2

1

CASE 2

THE SILENT CANDIDATE

Jackson Towne, a new supervisor in accounting, has just conducted his first interview to fill a vacancy in his unit. The candidate, Joan Smith, seemed well qualified on paper but had so little to say during the interview that Jackson is concerned about her ability to communicate with other employees in the normal course of business. Joan answered most of his questions with a simple yes or no. She seemed impressed when he told her about his extensive background and accomplishments, but did not offer to share her own. She became flustered when he criticized the quality of the accounting curriculum at the college she attended, but did not challenge his remarks.

Why do you think the applicant remained silent? Check ✔ the answer, or answers, that seem the most likely reason to you.

☐ Joan Smith was shy.

☐ Her verbal skills were weak.

☐ She was intimidated by Jackson Towne.

☐ She wasn't feeling well.

☐ The questions Jackson Towne asked lent themselves to yes or no answers rather than a free flow of information.

☐ All of the above.

☐ None of the above.

Check your answer with the author's on page 66.

A candidate's willingness to share information is often directly proportionate to the questioning skill of the interviewer. Questioning skills are very important. You will learn in the next few pages, how to learn and apply these skills.

Take notes as necessary during the interview. Keep them pertinent, brief, and to the point.

USING PROBES IN INTERVIEWING

Probes can be used to learn more about an applicant's thoughts and feelings without biasing the answers.

Here are some examples of commonly used probes.

PROBE	PURPOSE OR TECHNIQUE	EXAMPLE (Interviewer's Response in Boldface)
Clarifying	An attempt to determine the meaning of a response.	"A person who is not part of the 'in' group can't expect an increase. **"What do you mean by 'in' group?"**
Neutral response	An expression by the interviewer to encourage more information without biasing it.	"It sounded good at the time." **"Uh-huh."** "It didn't turn out that way though." **"Could you explain what you mean?"**
Silence	The interviewer looks expectantly at the applicant but does not speak.	"You know I think they took advantage of me?" **Silence—5 to 10 seconds.** "Yeah, they promised me a promotion but I never got it."
Expanding	Seeking new information to build on a previous statement.	"I was beginning to pick up vibrations that my job might be phased out." **"Uh-huh. What vibrations?"**
Repeating	Persisting in getting an answer to the question already asked but not answered.	**"Which of your qualifications contributed to your promotion?"** "Well, you see the old supervisor retired so the job was open." **"I see, but which of your qualifications contributed to your promotion?"**

PROBE	PURPOSE OR TECHNIQUE	ILLUSTRATION OF PROBE (Interviewer's Response in Boldface)
Clarifying inconsistencies	Reflecting that what the applicant has just said is inconsistent with a previous statement.	''That being the case, I decided to look for another job.'' **''I'm sorry, I seem to be confused. I thought you left that job to finish your analytical training. What gave me that impression?''**
Confirming feelings	A statement by the interviewer expressing what he or she believes the applicants intended meaning to be.	''I didn't get any credit for the new system even though it was my idea and I worked over 1,000 hours on it.'' **''You feel your creativity and willingness to work long hours are not appreciated?''**
Summarizing key ideas	An effort by the interviewer to summarize the last few applicant responses.	''So basically it was my baby all the way.'' **''It was your idea, you sold it to top management, and then worked out all the details, including implementation. Right?''**

Now take a minute to practice with questions. The next page lists five areas an interviewer might wish to explore with an applicant. In each area, write one non-directive and one directive question you feel would be helpful in obtaining useful information about an applicant's background. Although your questions will be different, you can check your approach with those of the author on page 66.

PRACTICING WITH QUESTIONS

Complete the exercise below by creating one non-directive and one directive question you would ask an applicant.

AREAS TO BE EXPLORED	OPEN ENDED NON-DIRECTIVE QUESTION	DIRECTIVE QUESTION
Previous Employment		
College or University		
Interest In The Position		
Unique Qualifications		
Personal Goals		

44

THE APPLICANT NEEDS INFORMATION TOO.

Before you can reach second base, and before you conclude the interview, it is essential the applicant's need for information be satisfied. The next page will suggest ways to accomplish this, along with some ideas on how to close the interview.

SATISFY THE APPLICANT'S NEED FOR INFORMATION

A candidate needs information to adequately assess the job and the organization. This includes specific job requirements; working hours; starting date; salary and benefits; as well as something about the organization, and its people. (See Appendix B for tips.)

The best time to discuss these items in any detail is toward the end of the interview. One reason for this is because the interviewer wants an applicant's responses to questions to be unbiased and spontaneous—not influenced by what the applicant thinks he or she wants to hear. Some candidates are adept at saying exactly what the interviewer has unknowingly coached them to say.

As soon as both parties have the information they need, the interviewer should bring the interview to a close. An excellent way to accomplish this is when the interviewer:

1. Assesses the applicant's interest in the position.

2. Informs the applicant where things stand and what the next steps will be.

3. Insures the candidate understands when a decision will be made and how he or she will be notified.

4. Thanks the interviewee for his or her time and closes the session on a positive note.

> REMEMBER TO FOLLOW THROUGH! EVERY APPLICANT DESERVES AN ANSWER AS SOON AS IT CAN BE PROVIDED.

46

**CONGRATULATIONS—YOU HAVE
REACHED SECOND BASE!**

Before starting for third, complete the case
study on the facing page.

CASE 3

THE UNPRODUCTIVE SALESPERSON

Mike Williams, District Sales Manager for BioTech, recently hired Norm Peterson to handle the Middletown sales territory. The vacancy occurred unexpectedly and Mike, feeling the territory should be covered as quickly as possible, only interviewed one candidate. Norm Peterson looked so good on paper and was so friendly during the interview, Mike felt it was unnecessary to look further. Although Mike felt he should have investigated Norm's academic credentials and prior sales record, he didn't because of the time required.

After three months, sales in Middletown declined fifteen percent although the potential market had increased. Mike checked with three former customers in the Middletown territory to learn why they were no longer buying from BioTech. All told him they had never met Norm Peterson, and assumed BioTech was no longer represented in the territory. Two others called Mike to complain that Norm refused to visit them because the volumes they were interested in buying weren't large enough to warrant his time.

When Mike raised these problems, Norm said he had been busy trying to close some big accounts and it wasn't worth his time to fool around with small accounts. When Mike pressed him for details, Norm became short tempered. Sales had been lost, Norm said, because a competitor had cut their prices.

What mistakes did Mike make in selecting Norm? Note them in the space below.

_____

_____

_____

_____

_____

You will find the author's answer on page 66.

PART III

EVALUATING THE CANDIDATES AND MAKING THE BEST DECISION

GENERAL PRINCIPLES GOVERNING APPLICANT EVALUATION

Following an interview, the applicant's qualifications must be objectively evaluated in terms of the position to be filled. Can the applicant do the job? Will the candidate make a positive contribution to the hiring organization? Four general principles govern evaluation. They include:

1. **Be Hypercritical.**
   The decision to hire is one of the most important decisions an organization will face. A poor decision will be expensive and painful to everyone concerned.

   Do not gloss over any basic weakness because you like some other less important qualification. If you notice a job related weakness (such as poor verbal skills in a customer relations applicant) during the interview, think how difficult it will be to live with once the person has been hired and is not nearly so anxious to please.

2. **Base Your Evaluation On Facts.**
   Compare qualifications against job requirements. Do not look for, or guess at, hidden meanings in the individual's responses or behavior. Be aware of behaviors that are likely to surface once on the job.

3. **Concentrate On Behavior, Not Words Alone.**
   Some interviewers are carried away by the applicant's words and overlook behavior. If a candidate is asked to describe their former supervisor, for example, there is no way of knowing how accurate that description is. What the applicant emphasizes however, can be important. An observer can learn much about the applicant's likes and dislikes, organizational skills, and general attitude by concentrating on both words *and* behavior.

4. **Seek Confirmation Of Your Evaluation.**
   Check your evaluation with other interviewers who talked to the same person. Check academic credentials with the granting institution. Talk to at least two previous employers. If references are listed, call them.

EVALUATE OBJECTIVELY

Objectivity is an essential quality when evaluating an applicant.

For example, handicapped people often produce more high quality work than their non-handicapped colleagues. Older employees are frequently more reliable, productive and loyal than those who are younger. BE SURE YOU ARE EVALUATING THE RIGHT THINGS!

The next page suggests some ways in which objectivity can be achieved.

HOW TO EVALUATE CANDIDATES OBJECTIVELY

There are several ways to maintain objectivity when evaluating prospective employees. They include the following. Check ✔ those you agree are important.

☐ 1. Evaluate the extent of the applicant's experience and the effectiveness of past performance against your job requirements. Are both acceptable? Try to remember that ten years of experience is quite different from one year of experience ten times. Focus on what was accomplished in past jobs.

☐ 2. Determine the level of responsibility previously held by the applicant. Is it about the same? More? Less? Can the applicant make the transition to the position in question?

☐ 3. Examine the skill and knowledge level of the applicant. Are they adequate to meet your needs? Are they adaptable to your job?

☐ 4. Identify the applicant's strengths. Are they adaptable? Will they enhance the position in question?

☐ 5. Determine the applicant's weaknesses. Would they have a negative effect on performance, or be inconsequential?

☐ 6. Evaluate indicators of stability and progress. Can you reasonably project the future based on the past record? Are stability and progress important to the job?

☐ 7. Will the applicant be compatible with others in the work group?

☐ 8. Probe the history of the candidate to determine past dependability, productivity, and attitude toward work, co-workers, supervision and customers.

☐ 9. Check all references carefully. In addition, verify all dates of employment, jobs held, academic institutions attended, degrees conferred and special honors awarded. (See Appendix C for tips.)

MAKE RATIONAL DECISIONS

Most people have prejudices. Interviewers must recognize theirs, and neutralize them during a job interview.

Physical appearance, clothing and personal mannerisms often play too large a role in the selection of a candidate. Guard against having one negative cause you to overlook the positives. Similarly do not allow one positive to blind you to the negatives.

It is important to:
• evaluate all applicants by the same
    criteria.
• be aware of your equal opportunity
    goals.
• not violate Federal, State or Local laws.
• give all candidates the same
    consideration.

Try to compare applicants to the job—not one against the other. A form like the one on the next page can help you do this.

COMPARE APPLICANTS TO THE JOB

COMPARISON OF CANDIDATES TO POSITION REQUIREMENTS

POSITION TO BE FILLED___*Typist/Community Health Education*___

Rate each candidate using the following scale.

1. Knowledge and/or skill level well below position requirements.
2. Knowledge and/or skill level meet minimum position requirements.
3. Knowledge and/or skill level meet all position requirements.
4. Knowledge and/or skill level unusually extensive and useful in this position.
5. Knowledge and/or skill level exceed position requirements.

Circle the name of the candidate selected.

CANDIDATES

	S.G. Jerome	P.R. Parker	N.S. Sherman	A.P. Norman	
General Knowledge Requirements:	RANKING				
1. *Community Health Education Functions*	*1*	*2*	*4*	*2*	
2.					
3.					
4.					
5.					
Specific Job Skills and/or Knowledge:					
1. *Typing—55 wpm*	*3*	*3*	*3*	*3*	
2. *Spelling & Grammar*	*2*	*3*	*3*	*3*	
3. *Basic Math Skills*	*1*	*3*	*4*	*2*	
4. *Page layout*	*3*	*3*	*4*	*3*	
5.					
Administrative Skills and/or Knowledge:					
1. *Filing & Filing Systems*	*2*	*3*	*4*	*3*	
2. *Office Machines*	*2*	*3*	*3*	*3*	
3. *Office Procedure & Practice*	*2*	*3*	*4*	*3*	
4.					
5.					
Attitude	*3*	*3*	*4*	*4*	
TOTALS	19	26	33	26	

PART IV

REVIEWING WHAT HAS BEEN LEARNED

Once you complete the evaluation of candidates, you have rounded third base and are headed for home!

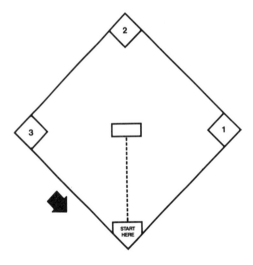

**YOU SCORE WHEN YOU SELECT
THE BEST POSSIBLE
CANDIDATE AVAILABLE!**

Your ultimate goal of selecting the best person will be fulfilled if you properly obtained information; gave information; evaluated data; drew conclusions; and made the right decision. Review the process on the next page.

REVIEW OF THE
DYNAMICS OF INTERVIEWING*

Schematically, the task of the interviewer looks like this:

INPUT	PROCESS	RESULTS
Job specifications Interview plan Information from candidate. Information given to candidate	Weigh information and conclusions against job specifications.	Fill job with best qualified candidate.

FOLLOWING IS WHAT THE AUTHOR FEELS IS THE BEST APPROACH

CONTRIBUTORS TO POSITIVE INPUTS	PROCESS POSITIVES	POSITIVE OUTCOMES
Thorough preparation of job specifications. Interviewer prepares interview plan.	Candidate qualifications measured against directly related job criteria.	Candidates selected or rejected for job related reasons.
Interviewer probes for data in critical areas.	Conclusions about candidate formed using appropriate data.	Candidate feels qualifications fully presented.
Interviewer listens 80 percent of time.	Candidate presents pertinent data about experience, knowledge and values.	Candidate feels what he or she has to say is important.
Use of open ended questions to stimulate the candidate.	The interviewer seems open and interested. The candidate opens up.	Decisions are based on a broad range of pertinent data.
Questions are free of suggestions of bias or prejudice.	The focus of the interview is consistently on the job.	Decisions are based on job related facts, not whim or caprice.
Interviewer gives an honest description of the position, the organization and related factors.	Candidate has full opportunity to learn about position.	Candidate is properly prepared to make a decision concerning degree of interest in position.

* This may either be read now, or as you prepare for your next interview.

DOCUMENTATION OF THE SELECTION PROCESS IS IMPORTANT

An interviewer must be able to demonstrate that all candidates for a position were evaluated on the same basis, and also show criteria used were directly job related. If supporting documentation cannot be produced, discrimination complaints may be impossible to defend.

A form similar to the one on the next page can be useful in documenting decisions. It should be supported by an accurate set of job specifications to which the applicant's qualifications have been compared.

DOCUMENT DECISIONS

CANDIDATE DISPOSITION

Use of this form helps demonstrate adherence to equal employment opportunity guidelines by documenting reasons decision was made to employ or reject a candidate. Such decisions must be based on valid, directly related job criteria applied consistently to all candidates. The following reasons for rejecting candidates are acceptable so long as the same statement cannot be applied to the person selected.

1. Does not meet minimum job specifications.
2. Meets minimum specifications, but not best qualified.
3. No prior related experience.
4. Less prior related experience than person selected.
5. Cannot meet physical standards for the position.
6. Lower level of required skills than person selected.

7. Less directly related training than candidate chosen.
8. Cannot work the schedule or hours required.
9. Applicant withdrew from consideration.
10. Other (List job related reason):

_____

_____

CANDIDATE: *S.G. Jerome*   POSITION APPLIED FOR: *Typist*

DATE: *11/30*   *Community Health Education*

Job offer will ( ) will not (✓) be extended.

Job related reason candidate selected was best qualified:

Four years directly related experience in a comparable community

health education position.

Directly job related reason this candidate was not selected. Insert appropriate number from the list above: *4*

Let all candidates know the status of their application as soon as possible. Those not employed may be told, ''The candidate whose qualifications best fit the job specifications was selected.''

CONGRATULATIONS!

You have rounded the bases in good form!
Now it's time to apply what you have learned.
You can do so by responding to the case study
on the next page.

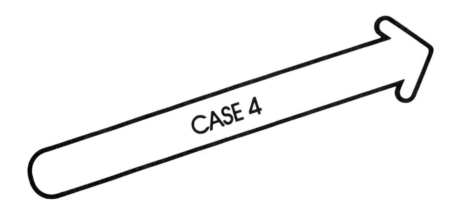

WHAT SHOULD YOU TELL JOY JENSEN?

Joy Jensen has just been employed to supervise a new section that is being added to your department. The work to be performed is totally new to you and your organization. All you have to guide you at this point is a mission statement. Joy is the only person in the organization with previous experience (from a former employer) in this particular function.

Joy is anxious to start staffing. She wants to begin interviewing candidates for the three to five positions she feels will be required to get the job done. She has had very little experience interviewing and selecting people.

What guidance should you give Joy about how she should begin to carry out the process? Write your suggestions below.

_____

_____

_____

_____

_____

_____

_____

_____

_____

You will find the author's response on page 67.

SEVEN PITFALLS TO AVOID

Check ✓ those you intend to avoid.

☐ 1. Failure to prepare (or review) the current job description as well as the job requirements for the vacancy to be filled.

☐ 2. Beginning an interview without an interview plan.

☐ 3. Permitting interruptions during the interview.

☐ 4. Failure to probe for objective evidence of the candidate's skills; knowledge; past successes and failures; dependability; attitude toward work, co-workers, supervision and customers.

☐ 5. Violation of equal employment opportunity laws.

☐ 6. Failure to share vital job information with the candidate.

☐ 7. Biased evaluation of candidate qualifications.

READING REVIEW

Please answer the following true-false questions.

True	False

_____ _____ 1. Current job descriptions and job specifications are the base point for beginning the selection process.

_____ _____ 2. The best time to review a candidate's application is during the interview.

_____ _____ 3. An interview is one appointment for which you can be late.

_____ _____ 4. It is a good idea to spend ten to fifteen minutes establishing rapport.

_____ _____ 5. The interviewer should be listening about eighty percent of the time.

_____ _____ 6. Applicants can be encouraged to elaborate on their answers by silence or non-committal remarks.

_____ _____ 7. You can probe for detailed information by asking pointed questions.

_____ _____ 8. Asking questions that can be answered "yes" or "no" save time and make evaluation easier.

_____ _____ 9. When making a selection decision, compare candidates to job specifications, not one another.

_____ _____ 10. The best interview style is called "interrogation."

_____ _____ 11. If an applicant asks questions, you should say, "I'll ask the questions, you answer them."

_____ _____ 12. All applicants need to know how their application will be handled and the outcome of the interview.

_____ _____ 13. The interviewer should take brief notes on key points.

_____ _____ 14. Rejected applicants should be told why in detail.

_____ _____ 15. The interviewer has a responsibility to tell candidates about the job and the organization.

_____ _____ 16. Bias and prejudice must be avoided at all times.

_____ _____ 17. The applicants skills are very important but so are attitudes, motivation and values.

_____ _____ 18. You should begin the interview by challenging candidates to prove they can do the job.

_____ _____ 19. How you document your selection decision is important.

_____ _____ 20. The interviewer should lead the interview, yet get the full participation of the applicant.

Turn to the next page and compare your answers with those of the author.

READING REVIEW ANSWERS

1. TRUE—They are both essential to quality selections.
2. FALSE—The best time is before the interview begins.
3. FALSE—An interview is as important as any other business appointment.
4. FALSE—Rapport can be established in five minutes or less.
5. TRUE—How else can you acquire the information you need?
6. TRUE—Silence tells the interviewee you are waiting to hear more.
7. TRUE—Probes help you with evasive, vague or sketchy replies.
8. FALSE—Yes and no answers may save time but they make evaluation impossible.
9. TRUE—Job qualifications count the most.
10. FALSE—Interrogations tend to make applicants tense, anxious and withdrawn.
11. FALSE—Respond appropriately with answers.
12. TRUE—Applicants also need to make plans and consider options.
13. TRUE—Notes are helpful in evaluating candidates.
14. FALSE—Tell them ''the best qualified applicant was selected.''
15. TRUE—Applicants also need information for decision making.
16. TRUE—Objective criteria lead to the best decision.
17. TRUE—Skills are essential but the person must also want to apply them.
18. FALSE—Interviewing is not an adversary process.
19. TRUE—It may make the difference in winning or losing a discrimination complaint.
20. TRUE—A good guide gets full participation in critical areas.

REFLECT FOR A MOMENT ON WHAT YOU HAVE LEARNED— THEN DEVELOP A PERSONAL ACTION PLAN USING THE GUIDE ON THE NEXT PAGE.

DEVELOP A PERSONAL ACTION PLAN

DEVELOP A PERSONAL ACTION PLAN

Think about the material you have read. Review the self-analysis questionnaire. Re-read the case studies and the reinforcement exercises. What did you learn about interviewing and the selection process? What did you learn about yourself? How can you apply what you learned? Make a commitment to become better at interviewing and evaluating candidates. Design a personal action plan to help you accomplish this goal.

The following guide may help you clarify your goals and outline actions required to achieve them.

1. My current interviewing and evaluation skills are effective in the following areas:

_____

_____

_____

2. I need to improve my interviewing and evaluation skills in the following areas:

_____

_____

_____

3. My interviewing and evaluation skills improvement goals are as follows: (Be sure they are specific, attainable and measurable.)

_____

_____

_____

4. These people and resources can help me achieve my goals:

_____

_____

_____

5. Following are my action steps, along with a time table to accomplish each goal:

_____

_____

_____

VOLUNTARY CONTRACT

Sometimes our desire to improve personal skills can be reinforced by making a contract with a supervisor, spouse or friend. If you believe a contract would help you, use the form on the following page.

VOLUNTARY
CONTRACT*

I, _____ , hereby agree to
(Your name)

meet with the individual designated below within thirty days

to discuss my progress toward incorporating the interview

techniques and ideas presented in this program. The purpose

of this meeting will be to *review* areas of strength and

establish action steps for areas where improvement may

still be required.

_____
Signature

I agree to meet with the above individual on

_____
Month   *Date*   *Time*

at the following location.

_____

_____
Signature

*This agreement can be initiated either by you or your superior.
Its purpose is to motivate you to incorporate important
concepts and techniques into your daily activities. It also
provides a degree of accountability between you and your
employer.

AUTHOR'S SUGGESTED ANSWER TO CASES

Case 1—Mary Ann's Replacement Problem

Before Mary Ann begins the search for candidates, she will want to complete the other steps. A vacancy offers the opportunity to take actions that could be difficult when fully staffed. A study of the position itself, the needs of the unit now and in the future, and the needs of those serviced, may lead to a variety of conclusions. These could include: elimination of the position; realignment of duties and functions within the unit to provide better service; a change in knowledge and skill requirements for the position; or a decision to cross-train existing staff.

If there are functional changes ahead for the unit, this may be the ideal time to begin acquiring the new skills and knowledge that will be required. If Mary Ann concludes the incumbent should be replaced by a person of similar qualifications, she can begin the selection process with confidence she understands the position requirements and has fully considered her options.

Case 2—The Silent Candidate

The applicant appears to have been intimidated by Jackson Towne's approach to the interview, and his desire to impress her with his own qualifications. Questions that can be answered only yes or no are the responsibility of the interviewer and will not encourage employees to elaborate their answers. Jackson should strive to be less intimidating and learn to use questions to his advantage.

Case 3—The Unproductive Salesperson

Mike Williams made a number of mistakes in selecting Norm Peterson. He let an unexpected vacancy stampede him into making a quick decision rather than a quality selection. He interviewed only one candidate thereby eliminating any opportunity to choose from a broader range of experience and talent. Mike rushed through the interview without probing for objective evidence of Norm's success in previous sales assignments; dedication to his work; attitude toward satisfying the needs of customers; and initiative and drive in running a sales territory. Mike also postponed checking on Norm's academic credentials and sales performance with previous employers until it was too late. If Mike had given this vacancy the priority it deserved, and taken the time to fully establish and evaluate Norm's qualifications he would not be faced with this mistake.

Case 4—What should you tell Joy Jensen?

Since Joy has experience in the work she will be supervising, she may believe she knows all of the skill requirements and will not need to prepare formal job descriptions and job specifications. Beginning to interview without these items would be dangerous from both an organizational, and legal point of view. It is too easy to overlook key requirements, or violate equal employment opportunity guidelines when operating from memory rather than documentation. Preparing job descriptions will help Joy get her organization and staffing needs in perspective and identify the critical qualifications required. She will also be able to more accurately determine how many people and what skill mix will be required to get the job done. She may discover the assignment can be achieved with only three people. Her supervisor or the personnel department can help.

In addition, as supervisor you would find it well worth the time and expense to provide Joy with some interview training and practice before her first interview. This will help avoid poor selection decisions and avoid illegal practices. With effort, Joy will be able to approach her task with confidence.

AUTHOR'S RESPONSE TO PRACTICING WITH QUESTIONS

AREAS TO BE EXPLORED	OPEN ENDED NON-DIRECTIVE QUESTION	DIRECTIVE QUESTION
Previous Employment	Why do you think you were so successful in your last job?	When did you get your last salary increase?
College or University	Why did you elect to major in math?	What was your grade point average?
Interest In The Position	How did you happen to become interested in this job?	Does this job appeal to you enough to start at a lower salary?
Unique Qualifications	What qualifications do you feel you have that uniquely qualify you for this position?	Can you give me two unique qualifications you would bring to this job?
Personal Goals	What goals have you set for yourself for the next two or three years?	Which goal do you expect to attain first?

APPENDIX A
DISCRIMINATORY OR NON-DISCRIMINATORY—
THAT IS THE QUESTION

A number of questions are listed below. Some may be legal, some may be illegal, some may be an unjustifiable invasion of the individual's privacy and some may suggest a pattern of discrimination. Read each question and then write your analysis in the space provided to the right of the question. You can check your analysis with the author's on page 71.

QUESTIONS   ANALYSIS

1. What part of the city do you live in? _____

2. Do you have any problem with working on religious days? _____

3. How many years of work experience do you have? _____

4. Have you ever been arrested? _____

5. Have you ever been convicted? _____

6. Are you single, married or divorced? _____

7. What languages do you speak fluently? _____

8. How old are you? _____

9. What are the ages of your children? _____

10. Who recommended you to us? _____

11. This position requires extensive travel, do you think you could handle it? _____

12. What does your spouse do? _____

APPENDIX A
DISCRIMINATORY OR NON-DISCRIMINATORY—
THAT IS THE QUESTION (Continued)

QUESTIONS	ANALYSIS
13. What would you do if your spouse were transferred?	_____
14. Have you made arrangements to have your children taken care of while you work?	_____
15. Do you plan to get married soon?	_____
16. Would you be comfortable supervising men?	_____
17. Have you ever been hospitalized? If so, for what?	_____
18. Have you had a major illness in the last five years?	_____
19. Are you taking prescribed drugs?	_____
20. Have you ever filed for Worker's Compensation Insurance?	_____
21. Have you ever been treated for drug addiction or alcoholism?	_____
22. Do you drink liquor or smoke?	_____
23. Do you own an automobile?	_____
24. What are your political preferences?	_____

THE BEST WAY TO AVOID ASKING INAPPROPRIATE QUESTIONS IS TO FIRST ASK YOURSELF IF THEY ARE REALLY DESIGNED TO OBTAIN JOB RELATED INFORMATION. IF THEY ARE NOT, DO NOT ASK THEM.

APPENDIX A
DISCRIMINATORY OR NON-DISCRIMINATORY— THAT IS THE QUESTION (Continued)

AUTHOR'S ANALYSIS

1. This question is not job related and has nothing to do with job performance. It could be construed to be an attempt to obtain ethnic background information since many neighborhoods are made up of persons of similar origins.

2. You cannot inquire into religious background. However, you can state what the normal work hours and days are and ask if there is any problem with working those hours and days.

3. This question might be considered age related and a problem if you tend to eliminate applicants in the 40-70 age range. Ask instead how many years of related job experience the applicant has had.

4. This question violates federal, state and many city laws and has been ruled inappropriate by most compliance agencies. Statistics indicate minorities have been arrested more than non-minorities, therefore, it could have an adverse impact on minority applicants.

5. You are allowed to ask if the applicant has been convicted of an offense if the question is job related, i.e., if applicant was convicted of embezzlement and is applying for a job as treasurer.

6. Not necessarily discriminatory, but if asked mostly of women it could have discriminatory implications. It would be difficult to show relevancy to job qualifications for either sex.

7. Poorly phrased. If you are looking for a specific language capability to meet a specific job requirement, it is better to ask, ''What degree of fluency do you possess in ?''.

8. Questions about an applicant's age could be viewed as discriminatory, especially when the applicant is in the ''protected age group'' − (40−70). It would be preferable to obtain age information after employment for a separate record for pension and insurance purposes.

9. This question is not job related and should not be asked.

10. The question itself is not a problem, but your hiring practices may be if you depend on employee referral and have a predominantly white, male, christian or youthful staff.

11. This question is all right if travel is part of the job requirement.

12. Could be discriminatory if asked only of women. Should only be asked if relevant to the job opening. Inquiring about the spouse's job would be relevant if there were a potential conflict of interest and then the question should be specific, i.e., ''Would working here pose any problem with your spouse's business interests?''

APPENDIX A

DISCRIMINATORY OR NON-DISCRIMINATORY— THAT IS THE QUESTION (Continued)

AUTHOR'S ANALYSIS (Continued)

13. Not discriminatory if asked equally of men and women. It is dangerous, however, since the traditional stereotype is that women follow their husbands' career. A woman might feel that she had been discriminated against if other questions were in the same vein.

14. The same reasoning applies here as in question number 13.

15. Poor question, especially if asked only of female applicants. Questionable relevance.

16. Poor question. Any question asked of one sex and not the other, puts the onus on you to prove you're not discriminating. Just ask if the applicant is comfortable supervising.

17. Under The Americans With Disabilities Act, pre-employment questions about illness may not be asked because they may reveal the existence of disability. However, an employer may provide information on its attendance requirements and ask if an applicant will be able to meet these requirements.

18. Same reasoning as that applied in question number 17.

19. Questions about the use of prescription drugs before a conditional job offer are not permitted because the answers might reveal the existence of certain disabilities.

20. You may not ask about an applicant's worker's compensation history prior to an offer, but may obtain such information after making a conditional job offer. Such questions are prohibited because they might reveal the existence of a disability. It is discriminatory under The Americans With Disabilities Act not to hire an individual with a disability because of speculation that the individual will cause increased worker's compensation costs.

21. This information cannot be requested because The Americans With Disabilities Act protects people addicted to drugs who have been successfully rehabilitated from discrimination.

22. Questions concerning personal habits, finances and politics are unjustifiable invasions of personal privacy unless related to job success.

23. Same reasoning that applied in question number 22.

24. Same reasoning that applied in questions number 22 and 23.

APPENDIX B
INFORMATION NEEDED BY THE APPLICANT

Part of the interviewer's job is sharing information about the position and the organization with the applicant. It's a two way street. You are evaluating the applicant and the applicant is evaluating you and the organization as a potential employer. You will want to present important job details and the organizations best points. In addition, you should have a basic information packet to give every candidate at the conclusion of the interview. Make sure the material is professional and polished. You will most likely reserve your strongest sales presentation for the most qualified candidates, but every applicant should leave the interview feeling well informed.

Be prepared to respond to a variety of questions. The persons in whom you will be most interested will most likely include those who ask the toughest questions. They probably care the most and have done the most research.

PROVIDE A BROAD UNDERSTANDING OF THE JOB AND THE BUSINESS

- **Describe The Job Itself**

  Describe the key duties and responsibilities to the extent the candidate has a clear picture of what the job entails. Review the tasks a new hire will be expected to perform immediately as well as those to be done as quickly as they can be assimilated. Describe the kind of training and support that will be provided.

- **Discuss The Supervisor**

  To whom will the new employee report? What is that person's management style? How long has she/he been in the position? What are his/her outstanding strengths?

- **Describe The Work Setting**

  Where will the work be done? Will the new employee have a private office? What type of technology is in use? Will other employees be supervised?

- **State A Salary Range**

  While it is unnecessary to discuss a specific salary level during the early stages of the interview process, it is only fair to indicate the salary range being considered. If the rate for the position is fixed, tell the candidate the rate and why it is fixed. Benefits can be summarized during the early stages of screening and described in full if and when an offer is made.

APPENDIX B
INFORMATION NEEDED BY THE APPLICANT
(Continued)

- **Overview The Department In Which The Opening Exists**

  What is its purpose and function? How many employees work there? How does it relate to the balance of the organization?

- **Discuss The Company's Products And Operations**

  Understanding the nature of the business will help the applicant evaluate her/his interest in becoming a part of the organization. You cannot assume the candidate is familiar with what is manufactured or the services provided. What differentiates the products or services from those of the competition? Is the company privately or publicly held? How is the organization structured? What are its current primary goals? For the future?

- **Present Appropriate Facts And Figures**

  How profitable is the company? How large is the plant? How many people does the organization employ?

- **Close The Interview With Specific Details Of What Will Happen Next**

  The interviewee has invested time and effort in presenting herself/himself for your consideration and deserves to know how and when the hiring decision will be made. Even if you do not hire the candidate, it is wise to leave them with a positive attitude about you and the organization you represent.

APPENDIX C
CHECKING REFERENCES

One of the most difficult issues facing hiring managers today is reference checking. It is an essential element of the applicant selection/evaluation process but like other elements of employment activity it must be handled with care.

The corporate world is full of misinformation, misunderstanding, misgivings, rumors and fear of litigation arising from reference checking. Legislation enacted during the past few years caused many employers to decide not to check references because they feared being sued by unsuccessful candidates for employment. Recently however, a number of negligent hiring cases have been brought in which employers have been sued for not checking the references of their employees.

Hiring managers who understand that checking references is an essential part of the hiring process will continue to check references and will take care to do so legally. The risks of not checking are too great. For example, take the case of the reporter who was hired by a major newspaper because of her impressive, but unverified academic credentials. The paper learned later that she had none of the academic credentials claimed, but only after she won a Pulitzer Prize for a story which also proved to be a fake. There are literally thousands of these tragic stories which could be told.

REFERENCE CHECKING TECHNIQUES

- **Ask The Candidate For Professional And Business References**

  These should be people with whom the candidate has worked on a day to day basis. The ideal references are superiors, peers and subordinates with whom the candidate has worked within the last five to seven years. Asking the candidate to supply references by name solves several problems.

  1. It would be wise as a matter of course to have every candidate sign a waiver releasing both the prospective employer and its agents from any liability that might result from checking references. However, the courts have consistently held that by providing the names of prospective references to a possible employer the candidate is giving an implied waiver of the right to privacy.

  2. When the applicant provides the references, it is likely they have asked permission of the persons named. If so, the references will be expecting a call about the applicant and be much more receptive to answering questions about past job performance. If they refuse, go back to the candidate and ask them to either convince the reference to provide information or give you another reference.

APPENDIX C
CHECKING REFERENCES (Continued)

- **Train The Reference Checker**

  One of the concerns about candidate furnished references is that they will say only good things. Since this is a reasonable concern, the reference checker should be highly experienced and well trained in the art of asking productive questions. They should know the job to be filled well and be well versed in applicable laws and regulations. A core list of job related questions to be asked should be prepared in advance, but some probes will be prompted by the reference's responses. The more professionally the reference checker handles these questions the better.

- **Keep Questions On Target**

  Ask job related questions only. Inquiries about lifestyle and personal affairs is asking for trouble. Be consistent in asking all references the same key questions so that responses can be compared. While all questions should be consistent, inconsistencies in the responses from the reference should be pursued until clarity is achieved. Probe any response which arouses your curiosity. Ask open end questions like, ''How?'', ''What?'', ''When?'', ''Why?'' and use phrases like, ''Please tell me more.'' ''Then what happened?''

  Here are some typical questions that might be asked.

  - How long did Susan work for the organization?
  - What was her first position?
  - What was her position when she left?
  - What other positions did she fill while there?
  - What are her strengths? Weaknesses?
  - How would you describe her work ethic?
  - Would you re-hire? Why? Why not?
  - This is what she would be doing for this firm. How do you think her skills and abilities would fit this position?
  - What reservations should I have about hiring her?
  - Who else in your organization would be qualified to comment on her performance?
  - Why did she leave your organization?

- **Verify Educational Qualifications**

  Some candidates think nothing of listing schools they never attended and academic credentials they never received. Verifying them in advance may save embarrassment later.

APPENDIX D
BIBLIOGRAPHY AND RESOURCES

Books

Smart Hiring: The Complete Guide to Recruiting Eployees
Robert Wendover, 1989
Management Staff Press, Inc.
7500 E. Arapahoe Road
Englewood, Colorado 80112
(800) 227-5510

Robert Half On Hiring
Rober Half, 1985
Crown Publishers, Inc.
1 Park Avenue
New York, NY 10016

The Hiring Handbook
Darlene Orlov, Ed., 1986
Institute for Management
14 Plaza Road
Greenvale, NY 11548

Labor and Employment Law Desk Book
Gordon Jackson, 1986
Prentice-Hall, Inc.
Englewood Cliffs, NJ

Labor and Employment Law:
Compliance and Litigation
Frederick T. Golder, 1987
Callaghan & Company
3201 Old Glenview Road
Wilmette, IL 60091

Immigration Employment Compliance Handbook
A.T. Fragomen and S.C. Bell, 1987
Clark Boardman Company
435 Hudson Street
New York, NY 10014

Modern Personnel Forms
Deborah Launer, Rev. 1988
Warren Gorham & Lamont
210 South Street
Boston, MA 02111

The Law of the Workplace:
Rights of Employers and Employees
Frederick T. Golder, 1987
Callaghan & Company
3201 Old Glenview Road
Wilmette, IL 60091

Employment Law in the 50 States:
A Reference for Employees
CUE/NAM
1331 Pennsylvania Ave. NW
Suite 1500-North Lobby
Washington, DC 20004-1703

Drug Testing Legal Manual
Kevin B. Zeese, 1988
Clark Boardman Company, Ltd.
435 Hudson Street
New York, NY 10014

Employer's Complete Guide to Immigration
Howard David Deutsch, 1987
Prentice Hall Information Services
Paramus, NJ 07652

Your First 30 Days
Elwood Chapman
Crisp Publications

New Employee Orientation
Charles Cadwell
Crisp Publications

High Performance Hiring
Robert W. Wendover
Crisp Publications

APPENDIX D
BIBLIOGRAPHY AND RESOURCES (Continued)

Current Periodicals

HR Magazine
Society for Human Resource Management
606 N. Washington Street
Alexandria, VA 22314
(703) 548-3440

HR News
Society for Human Resource Management
606 N. Washington Street
Alexandria, VA 22314
(703) 548-3440

Personnel Journal
P.O. Box 2440
Costa Mesa, CA 92628
(714) 751-1883

Boardroom Reports
Box 1026
Millburn, NJ 07041

Inc.
38 Commercial Wharf
Boston, MA 02110
(617) 227-4700

Employment Practice Reference Sources
Bureau of National Affairs
1231 25th Street NW
Washington, DC 20037
(301) 258-1033

Bureau of Law and Business
64 Wall Street
Madison, CT 06443
1-800-553-4569
(203) 245-7448 (CT)

Commerce Clearing House
4025 W. Peterson Ave.
Chicago, IL 60646
(312) 583-8500

Dartnell, Inc.
4660 Ravenswood Ave.
Chicago, IL 60640
(312) 561-4000

EEOC
Publications Department
2401 "E" Street, NW
Washington, DC 20507
(202) 634-6922

Personnel Forms

Amsterdam Printing and Litho
Wallins Corner Road
Amsterdam, NY 12010
1-800-833-6231
1-800-342-6116 (NY State)

Dartnell, Inc.
4660 Ravenswood Ave.
Chicago, IL 60640
1-800-612-5463
(312) 561-4000 (IL)

Selectform, Inc.
Box 3045
Freeport, NY 11520
(516) 623-0400

Testing

E.F. Wonderlic & Associates
820 Frontage Road
Northfield, IL 60093
(708) 446-8900

ETS Test Collection
Educational Testing Service
Princeton, NJ 08541
(609) 921-9000

London House, Inc.
1550 Northwest Highway
Park Ridge, IL 60068
1-800-323-5923
(708) 298-7311 (IL)

APPENDIX D
BIBLIOGRAPHY AND RESOURCES (Continued)

John E. Reid & Associates
233 N. Michigan, Suite 1614
Chicago, IL 60601
1-800-621-4553
(312) 938-9200

Stanton Corporation
417 South Dearborn
Chicago, IL 60605
1-800-621-4552
(312) 922-0970

Employment History Verification

Fidelifacts
50 Broadway
New York, NY 10004
1-800-223-3140
(212) 425-1520 (NY)

Equifax Services, Inc.
1600 Peachtree Street, NW
Atlanta, GA 30309
1-800-327-5932

Verified Credentials, Inc.
4010 West 65th Street
Minneapolis, MN 55435
(612) 431-1811

NOTES

NOTES

NOTES

NOW AVAILABLE FROM CRISP PUBLICATIONS

Books • Videos • CD Roms • Computer-Based Training Products

Subject Areas Include:

Management

Human Resources

Communication Skills

Personal Development

Marketing/Sales

Organizational Development

Customer Service/Quality

Computer Skills

Small Business and Entrepreneurship

Adult Literacy and Learning

Life Planning and Retirement

CRISP WORLDWIDE DISTRIBUTION

English language books are distributed worldwide. Major international distributors include:

ASIA/PACIFIC

Australia/New Zealand: In Learning, PO Box 1051 Springwood QLD, Brisbane, Australia 4127
Telephone: 7-841-1061, Facsimile: 7-841-1580
ATTN: Mssrs. Gordon

Singapore: Graham Brash (Pvt) Ltd. 32, Gul Drive, Singapore 2262
Telephone: 65-861-1336, Facsimile: 65-861-4815
ATTN: Mr. Campbell

EUROPEAN UNION

England: Flex Training, Ltd. 9-15 Hitchin Street, Baldock, Hertfordshire, SG7 6AL
Telephone: 1-462-896000, Facsimile: 1-462-892417
ATTN: Mr. Willets

INDIA

Multi-Media HRD, Pvt., Ltd., National House, Tulloch Road, Appolo Bunder, Bombay, India 400-039
Telephone: 91-22-204-2281, Facsimile: 91-22-283-6478
ATTN: Mssrs. Aggarwal

MIDDLE EAST

United Arab Emirates: Al-Mutanabbi Bookshop, PO Box 71946, Abu Dhabi
Telephone: 971-2-321-519, Facsimile: 971-2-317-706

NORTH AMERICA

Canada: Reid Publishing, Ltd., Box 69559-109 Thomas Street, Oakville, Ontario Canada L6J 7R4.
Telephone: (905) 842-4428, Facsimile: (905) 842-9327

SOUTH AMERICA

Mexico: Grupo Editorial Iberoamerica, Serapio Rendon #125, Col. San Rafael, 06470 Mexico, D.F.
Telephone: 525-705-0585, Facsimile: 525-535-2009
ATTN: Señor Grepe

SOUTH AFRICA

Alternative Books, Unit A3 Sanlam Micro Industrial Park, Hammer Avenue STRYDOM Park, Randburg, 2194 South Africa
Telephone: 2711 792 7730, Facsimile: 2711 792 7787
ATTN: Mr. de Haas

Selected Crisp titles are available in 23 languages. For more information contact International Publishing Manager, Suzanne Kelly-Lyall at (415) 323-6100.